Fabulous Fiona Facts

Fiona was born 6 weeks early in the morning on January 24, 2017.

Fiona's parents are Bibi and Henry.

Fiona's birth weight was 29 pounds.

Fiona was the lightest hippo ever recorded. Most baby hippos weigh between 50 pounds and 120 pounds at birth.

Fiona received 24 hour intensive care when she was born.

Fiona went into the pool for the first time when she was two days old.

Fiona was named when she was a week old, her name means "fair."

Fiona became very dehydrated and needed the help of Cincinnati Children's Hospital to insert an IV.

Fiona began drinking from a bottle when she was less than 2 weeks old.

Fiona ate hay for the first time at around 6 weeks old.

Fiona has a birthmark on her right rear leg. It is a big pink blob.

Fiona weighed 200 pounds on Sunday April 30.

Fiona touched noses with her Bibi through wire mesh at just under 3 months old.

Fiona and her mother interacted without the wire mesh on Mother's Day.

It took 6 months for Fiona to be gradually introduced to both parents but finally, on July 14, the hippo family began getting along swimmingly! They even napped together which is normal hippo behavior.

Fiona was 6 months old on July 24 and weighed at least 375 pounds. She has come such a long way but still has a bit further to go to reach her mother's weight of almost 4,000 pounds!

Fabulous Fiona Mad Libs

Fill in the missing words, making it as funny,
crazy or serious as you like!

Fiona was born at the

....(noun). She likes to

drink...(noun) and has started

eating......................................(noun) that her mother

has already ....(verb). When she was two

days old she went in the pool but she cannot...........................

(verb). Fiona has a ....(noun) shaped like a

big pink ....(noun). Her name

means...(adjective). On Mother's

Day Fiona and her mother ....(verb). Did you

know that hippos ....(verb) to show

their enemies they are ready to ....(verb)?

Thankfully, Fiona is growing ....(adverb)

every day and we will be able to ....(verb)

her very soon!

Did you know that a male hippo can weigh up to 4,000 pounds?

Fabulous Fiona

How many words can you make from the word hippopotamus?

Did you know that the name hippopotamus means river horse?

Fabulous Fiona's Friends Jumble

Unjumble the words and draw a line to match the animals.

hyenahs	rabez
oryx	ioln
wildebeest	plardeo
lion	polestane
elephant	shhneay
giraffe	nocerhiosr
leopard	xryo
rhinoceros	peletanh
cheetah	beetsiewld
zebra	fifgrae
antelopes	hatchee

Did you know the skin of a hippopotamus is two and a half inches thick?

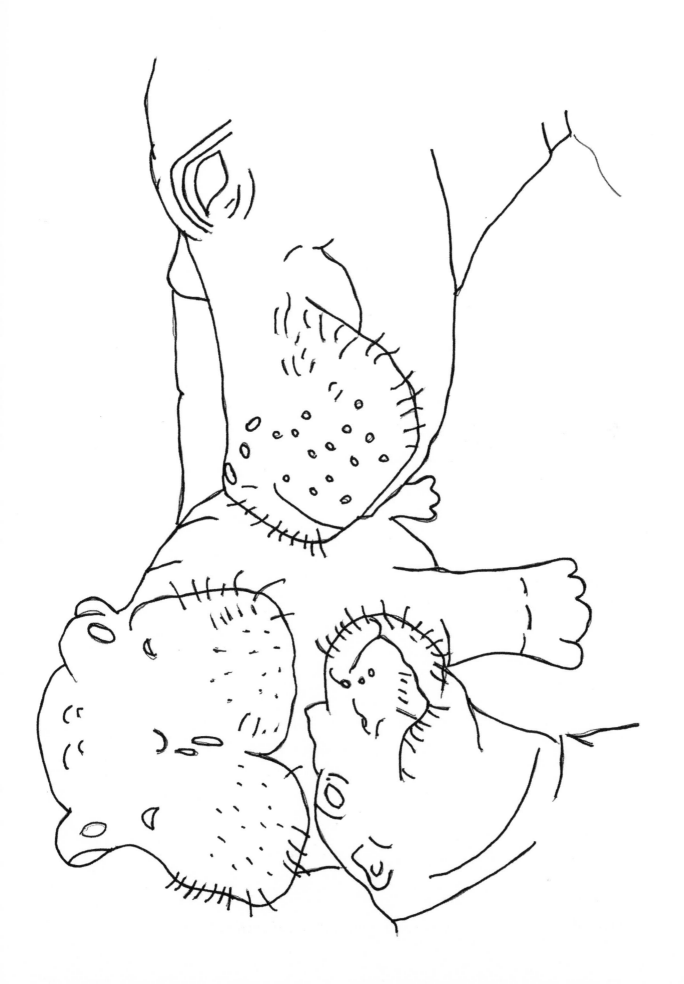

 # Fabulous Fiona postcard

Write Fiona a postcard and tell her all about yourself.

Dear Fiona	
	To Miss Fiona, The Cincinnati Zoo, Hippo Pool, 3400 Vine Street, Cincinnati, Ohio 45220

Did you know that hippos can store food in their stomachs and go three weeks without eating?

Fabulous Fiona

Draw a picture of Fiona here

Did you know that a hippopotamus closes its ears and nostrils when it dives underwater?

Join the dots then color Fabulous Fiona

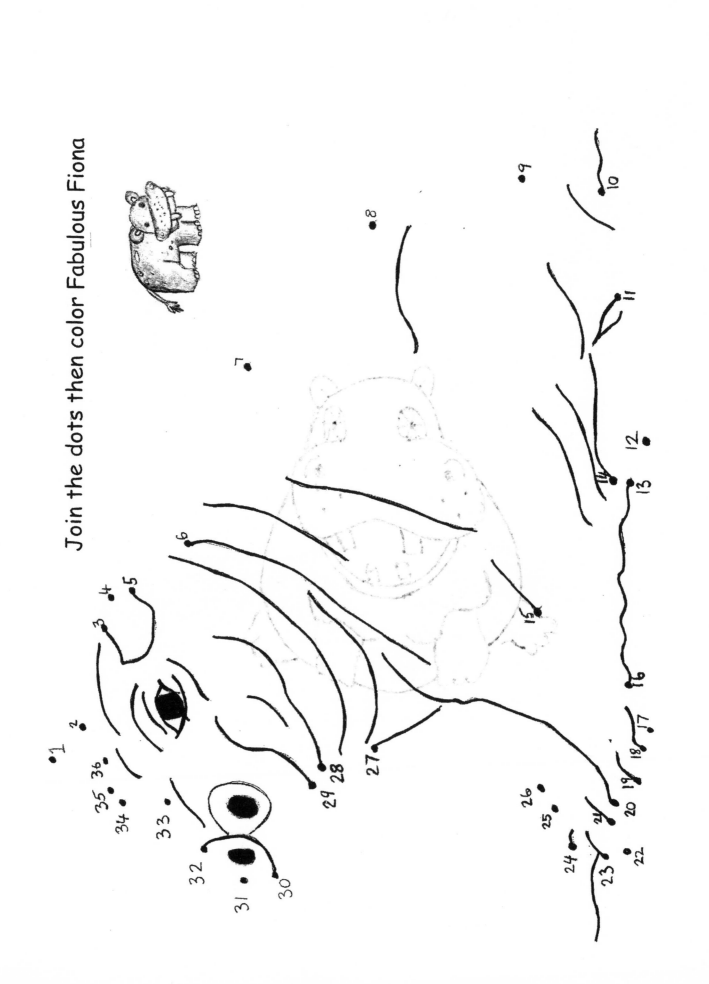

Fabulous Fiona Alphabet

Think of a word about Fiona for every letter of the alphabet. The first two have been done for you.

A Africa

B Bibi

C

D

E

F

G

H

I

J

K

L

M

N

O

P

Q

R

S

T

U

V

W

X

Y

Z

Did you know that the milk of a mother hippo is pink?

Fabulous Fiona comic strip

Make your own Fabulous Fiona comic strip

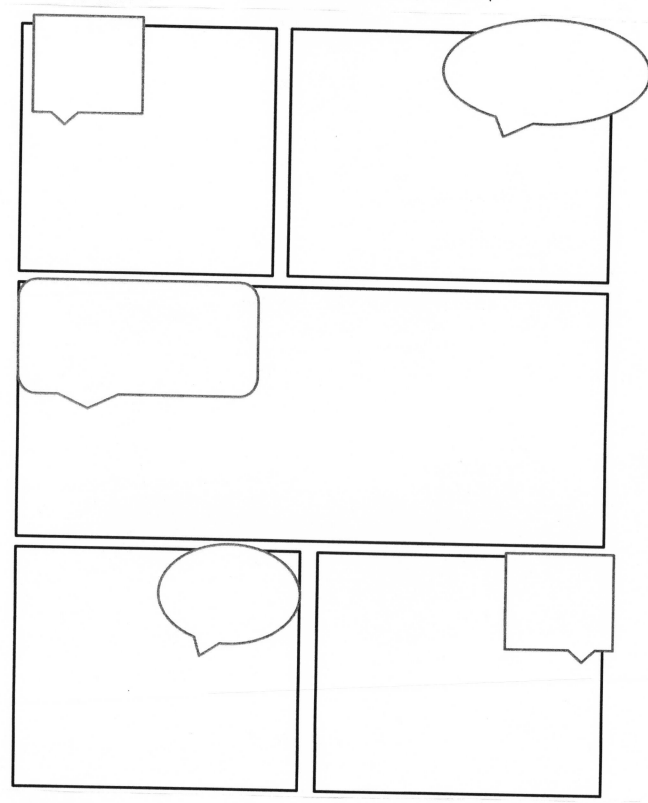

Did you know that a hippo's skin produces a red liquid that works like a moisturizer and a sunscreen?

Fabulous Fiona Hashtags

 How many more hilarious hashtags can you think of about Fiona?

Team Fiona

How many rolls?

Chunky chunky hippo

Did you know that hippos love to eat grass and in one night can eat up to 77 pounds of their favorite food?

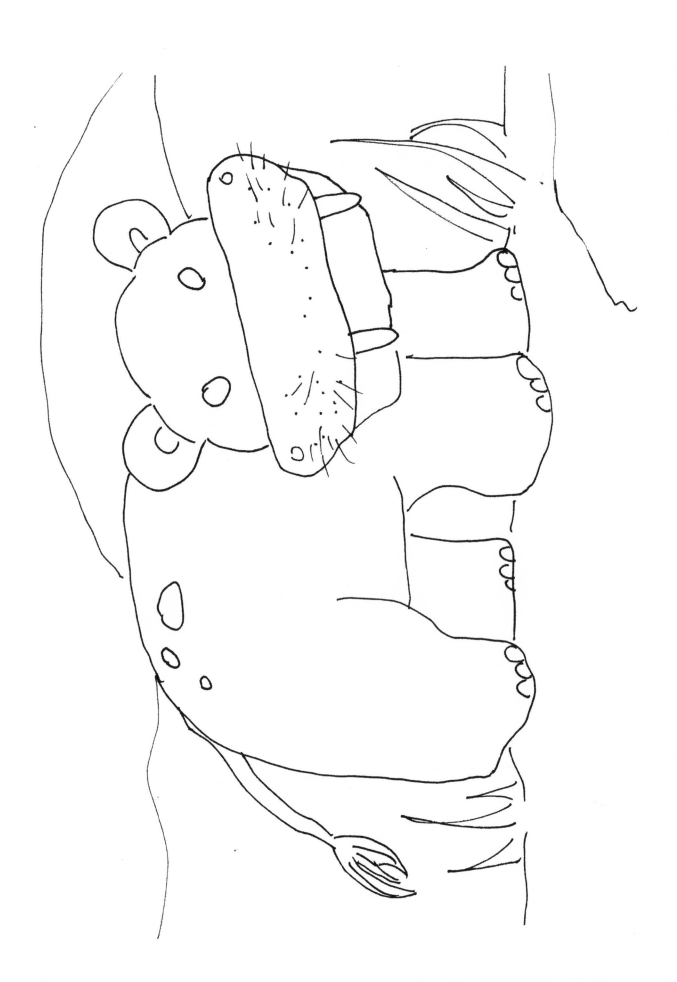

Fabulous Fiona Fantastic Facts

How many fantastic facts can you find out about hippos and Fabulous Fiona? Can you fill this page?

Did you know that a hippo yawns to show its enemy it is ready for a fight?

A group of Fabulous Fionas

A collection of hippos is known as a herd, pod or bloat.

Be an investigator and fill in the blanks about these crazy collections.

A .... of penguins.

A .... of geese.

A .... of jellyfish.

A .... of crows.

A .... of whales.

A parliament of ....

A battery of ....

A turn of ....

A congregation of ....

A pod of ....

Think about Fiona, devise a new description for a group of hippos.

A ....of hippos.

Did you know that another word for a group of hippos is a dale of hippos?

Roll a Fabulous Fiona

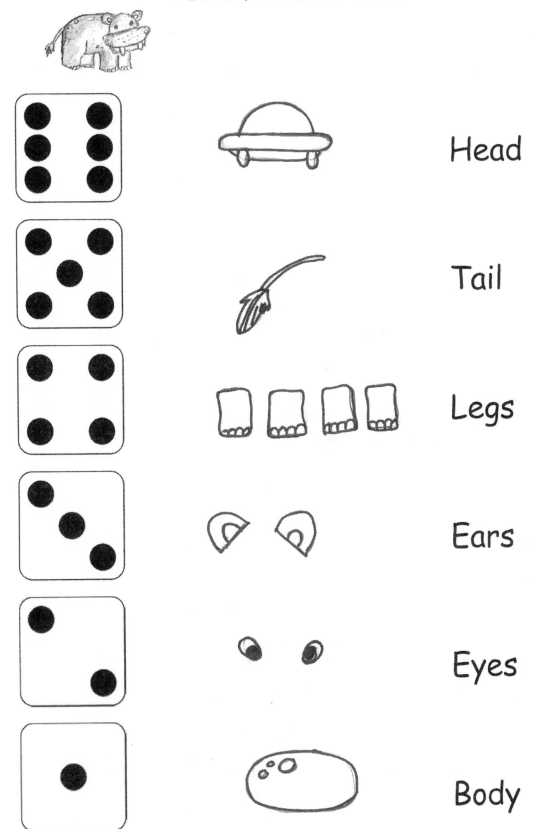

6 — Head

5 — Tail

4 — Legs

3 — Ears

2 — Eyes

1 — Body

Did you know that scientists believe hippos evolved around 55 million years ago?

Fabulous Fiona Tic Tac Toe

Play tic tac toe with Fiona and her friend Thomas the Turtle

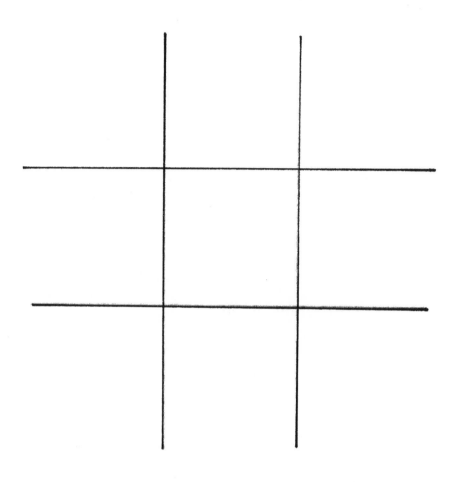

Did you know that the first hippo exhibited in a zoo was in London Zoo in 1850?

Fabulous Fiona Finish The Picture

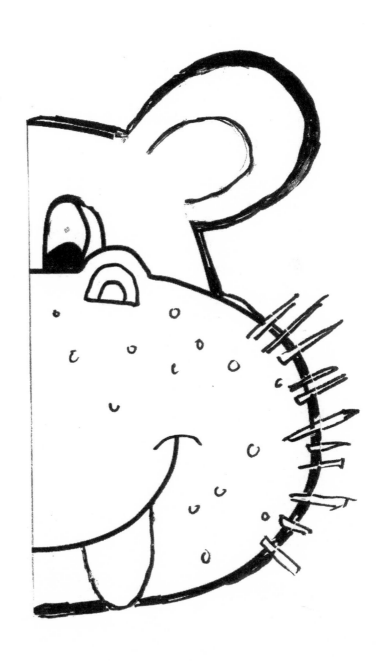

Did you know that a hippo's closest living relatives are whales and porpoises?

Fabulous Fiona Finish The Story

Choose one of these story starters and finish your own Fabulous Fiona story.

Fiona woke up very early one morning feeling extremely hungry. Bibi and Henry were still fast asleep and she did not want to wake them. She looked around and could not see any hay to eat when suddenly her friend Thomas the turtle opened his eyes and said............................

Fiona was having so much fun playing with Bibi in the pool when she heard a very strange laughing noise coming from the hyenas that lived nearby. The meerkats joined in with piercing squeals. Fiona's head peeped out of the pool and saw all the animals in the zoo running around free. What had happened?..

Fiona tossed and turned in her sleep. She was having a wonderful dream. She dreamed she was floating in a river in West Africa surrounded by other baby hippos when the roar of a lion startled them and they all ....

I woke up filled with excitement. Today I was going to the zoo to see Fiona for the first time. I couldn't wait to get there and was ready to go before anyone else in my family. I had no idea how my day of delight would change into a day of disaster.....................................

Did you know that a hippo has webbed toes to help paddle through water?

Fabulous Fiona Finish The Story

....
....
....
....
....
....
....
....
....
....
....
....
....
....
....
....
....
....
....
....
....
....
....
....

Did you know that a hippo stays in water to remain cool during the day but at night it leaves the water to eat grass?

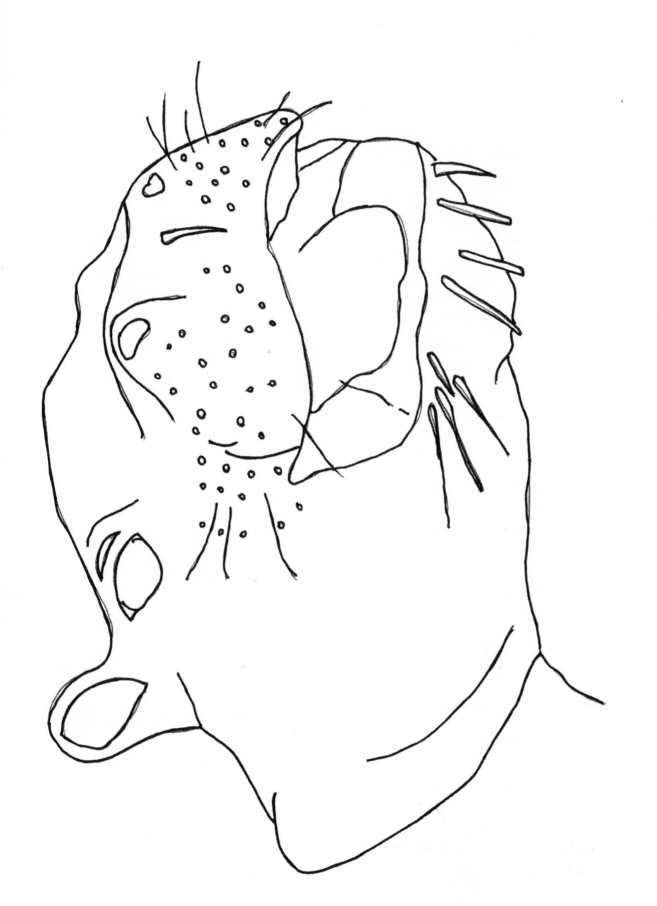

Fabulous Fiona Sudoku

	1		
2	3	1	
		4	
1		3	2

Have fun filling the grids so that each number is used just once in every row, column and box.

	4	5	6		2
6	2				
	5	6	1		3
		2	5		4
	3				
2		1	3		5

Did you know there are two types of hippopotamus? The common hippopotamus and the pygmy hippopotamus.

Fabulous Fiona And Her Animal Friends

Complete the crossword below

Across

3. Animals that eat both plants and meat
5. Animals that are active at night
8. "Cold-blooded" and live on land and water
11. Mammals that live in the ocean.
12. Has a spinal column
15. Animals that have a constant temperature
16. Breathe through gills and live in water
17. Our fabulous hippo
18. "Cold-blooded" and breathe with lungs
19. Animals that eat plants
20. Animals that are active during the day
21. "Warm-blooded" animals with feathers and wings

Down

1. Mammals that carry their babies in a pouch outside their bodies.
2. The city where Fiona was born
4. Fiona's mother
6. Does not have a spinal column
7. Animals whose body temperature changes with their environment
9. Fiona's father
10. "Warm-blooded" and are mostly born alive
13. Animals that eat meat
14. Animals that have large front teeth

Fabulous Fiona Wordsearch African Animals

```
q  h  z  p  t  g  i  r  a  f  f  e
l  i  o  f  f  g  o  h  t  r  a  w
c  p  w  x  x  l  h  c  s  s  l  j
h  p  o  a  n  t  e  l  o  p  e  m
e  o  v  n  r  v  l  g  r  l  o  g
e  p  w  i  l  d  e  b  e  e  s  t
t  o  u  b  f  d  p  r  c  a  e  h
a  t  s  k  q  h  h  q  o  l  v  y
h  a  z  e  b  r  a  d  n  a  o  e
s  m  p  w  v  h  n  h  i  p  e  n
v  u  u  a  i  m  t  v  h  m  p  a
x  s  j  v  l  i  o  n  r  i  r  k
```

hippopotamus	rhinoceros	giraffe	lion
elephant	antelope	cheetah	warthog
wildebeest	impala	hyena	zebra

Did you know that when a hippo is completely submerged in water its ears and nostrils fold shut to keep water out?

Help Fabulous Fiona Find Her Bottle!

Did you know that a male hippopotamus is a bull and a female is a cow?

Fabulous Fiona Mask

Color, cut, stick on card and you can be Fiona!

Fabulous Fiona Wordsearch

```
W F E R E P U D R Z Z L
C A L F Z A M Y B L O M
F A N X A F R H G M S N
I B I B I X I S A C H U
A G B Y U P F K Z T G W
N W U R P H I O G T O O
O H L O H L O H M C S C
I N L A F R I C A Y S V
F B H S T H U A B B A Z
V G J P M G G U O N R O
D U V Y R N E H O B G H
R P F M Q N F K U A K V
```

FIONA   GRASS   COW

AFRICA   BIBI   ZOO

HIPPO   CALF

Did you know that wild hippos live for around 40 years but in captivity they tend to live longer and may even reach 50 years?

Fabulous Fiona Crossword

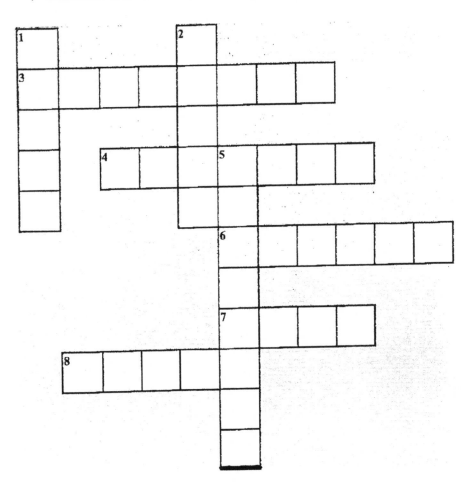

turtle   zebra   shark   elephant

antelope   hippo   giraffe   lion

Across

3. Has a trunk

4. Has a long neck

6. Has a shell

7. Has a large mane

8. Fiona is one

Down

1. Has black and white stripes

2. Great white or hammerhead

5. Looks like a deer

Did you know that a hippo can hold its breath for about five minutes?

Fabulous Fiona And The Hippos In Africa

The number of hippos in Africa is decreasing and they are considered "vulnerable."

Hippo meat is very popular, and in some cases essential, amongst the poor people in Africa and many hippos are killed for their meat.

The ivory from hippos (and also elephants) brings in a lot of money so many poachers kill hippos for their ivory.

Hippos are also killed to minimize human-wildlife conflict. 2,900 people, mainly in Africa, are killed each year by hippos. The hippo is considered to be the most dangerous large land animal in Africa. They have a huge mouth measuring up to 4 feet across and massive teeth and tusks. A male hippo can weigh up to 4,000 pounds.

Hippos need deep bodies of water and lots of green vegetation in order to thrive. They don't like sharing their environment with other animals and this makes it hard to conserve areas for them to live.

As the human population grows, new settlements and roads are built. This impacts wildlife habitats and hippos now mainly live in protected areas.

Hippos in captivity do well but it is dangerous to take one out of the wild and place it in captivity. Almost all of the hippos found in zoos today were born there.

Hippo conservation is vital to the health of African wetlands where the ecosystems have evolved with hippos living there in groups ranging from ten to hundreds. Without the hippo the habitat would have significant but unpredictable consequences.

It is estimated that there are between 125,000 and 150,000 common hippos and between 2,000 and 3,000 pygmy hippos in the wild.

Fabulous Fiona Answers

A group of Fabulous Fionas (answers may vary)

A huddle of penguins,
A gaggle of geese,
A smack of jellyfish,
A murder of crows,
A school of whales,
A parliament of owls,
A battery of barracuda,
A turn of turtles,
A congregation of crocodiles,
A pod of dolphins.

Fabulous Fiona and her animal friends

Across 3. Omnivores 5.Nocturnal
8.Amphibians 11.Cetaceans
12.Vertebrates 15.Warmblooded
16.Fish 17.Fiona 18. Reptiles
19. Herbivores 20. Diurnal
21. Birds

Down 1.Marsupials 2.Cincinnati
4.Bibi 6.Invertebrates
7.Coldblooded 9.Henry
10.Mammals 13.Carnivores
14.Rodents

Fabulous Fiona wordsearch African Animals

	h			g	i	r	a	f	f	e
	i			g	o	h	t	r	a	w
c	p					s				
h	p	a	n	t	e	l	o	p	e	
e	o				l		r			
e	p	w	i	l	d	e	b	e	e	s	t
t	o				p		c	a		h
a	t				h		o	l		y
h	a	z	e	b	r	a		n	a	e
	m				n		i	p		n
	u				t		h	m		a
	s			l	i	o	n	r	i	

Fabulous Fiona wordsearch

C	A	L	F								
						H					
	B	I	B	I		I					
A	B			P			Z			W	
N	U	P			O					O	
O	L	O			O				S	C	
I	L	A	F	R	I	C	A		S		
F									A		
									R		
		Y	R	N	E	H			G		

Fabulous Fiona crossword

Across 3.elephant 4.giraffe 6.turtle
7.lion 8.hippo **Down** 1.zebra 2.shark
5.antelope

Did you know that hippos are one of the noisiest animals in Africa? Some hippo noises are as loud as a rock concert!

Fabulous Fiona Sudoku Answers

4	1	2	3
2	3	1	4
3	2	4	1
1	4	3	2

1	4	5	6	3	2
6	2	3	4	5	1
4	5	6	1	2	3
3	1	2	5	6	4
5	3	4	2	1	6
2	6	1	3	4	5

Did you know that the hippopotamus is the third largest land animal? The elephant and the white rhinoceros are the largest.

We'd love to hear your thoughts on this book and all things Fiona!

Please email us at postman45202@gmail.com

Postman Productions

2017